THE SHERIFF OF ROTTENSHOT

Poems by   Jack Prelutsky

Pictures by   Victoria Chess

Greenwillow Books
New York

With a grin,

for Carolynn

Library of Congress Cataloging
in Publication Data

Prelutsky, Jack.
The sheriff of Rottenshot.
Summary: A collection of
sixteen humorous poems including
"The Sheriff of Rottenshot,"
"The Soggy Frog," and
"The Ghostly Grocer of
Grumble Grove."
1. Children's poetry, American.
2. Humorous poetry, American.
[1. American poetry.
2. Humorous poetry]
I. Chess, Victoria, ill.
II. Title.
PS3566.R36S5
811'.54   81-6420
ISBN 0-688-00205-6 AACR2
ISBN 0-688-00198-X (lib. bdg.)

CONTENTS

THE SHERIFF OF ROTTENSHOT

The sheriff of Rottenshot, Jogalong Jim,
wore a one-gallon hat with a ten-gallon brim.
He was short in the saddle and slow on the draw,
but he was the sheriff, his word was the law.

Jogalong Jim didn't know how to fight,
his boots were too big and his britches too tight,
he wasn't too bright and he wasn't too brave,
and he needed a haircut, a bath and a shave.

His rifle was rusty and couldn't shoot straight,
his bony old pony groaned under his weight.
The sheriff of Rottenshot, Jogalong Jim,
was lucky that nobody lived there but him.

PHILBERT PHLURK

The major quirk of Philbert Phlurk
was tinkering all day,
inventing things that didn't work,
a scale that wouldn't weigh,
a pointless pen that couldn't write,
a score of silent whistles,
a bulbless lamp that wouldn't light,
a toothbrush with no bristles.

He built a chair without a seat,
a door that wouldn't shut,
a cooking stove that didn't heat,
a knife that couldn't cut.
He proudly crafted in his shop
a wheel that wouldn't spin,
a sweepless broom, a mopless mop,
a stringless violin.

He made a million useless things
like clocks with missing hands,
like toothless combs and springless springs
and stretchless rubber bands.
When Phlurk was through with something new,
he'd grin and say with glee,
"I know this does not work for you,
but ah! it works for me."

KERMIT KEENE

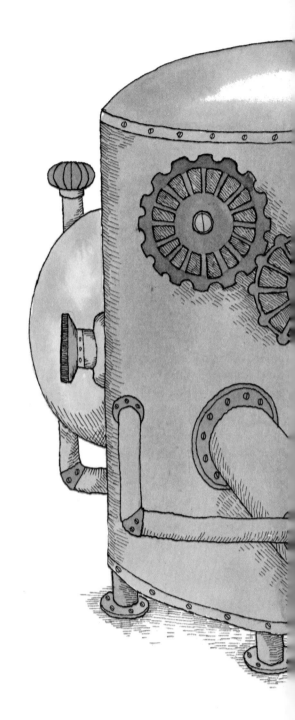

Kermit Keene, unkempt though clean,
devised a devilish machine.
"My gadget," he declared with pride,
"transforms whatever's placed inside."

He dropped a squirrel in the spout,
a pigeon popped directly out,
he plopped the pigeon right back in,
out squirmed a snake with shining skin.

The snake was traded for a cat,
a pekinese, a pig, a rat,
and shortly, in the rodent's place,
a rabbit occupied the space.

But when he put the rabbit back,
he gasped and screamed, "Oh no! Alack!"
for something monstrous, moist and mean
emerged and swallowed Kermit Keene.

THE CENTIPEDE

The centipede with many feet
is bicycling about the street,
she pedals at surprising speed
upon her odd velocipede.

The centipede with care has put
a pedal under every foot,
she rates awards, she merits medals,
working all those centipedals.

THE SOGGY FROG

The toad's abode
is by the road,
the frog's abode
is boggy—

explaining why
the toad seems dry,
and why the frog
seems soggy.

THE COURT JESTER'S LAST REPORT TO THE KING

Oh sire! My sire! your castle's on fire,
I fear it's about to explode,
a hideous lizard has eaten the wizard,
the prince has turned into a toad.

Oh sire! Good sire! there's woe in the shire,
fierce trolls are arriving in force,
there are pirates in port, monstrous ogres at court,
and a dragon has melted your horse.

Oh sire! Great sire! the tidings are dire,
a giant has trampled the school,
your army has fled, there are bees in your bed
and your nose has come off...... **APRIL FOOL!**

14

THE SPAGHETTI NUT

Eddie the spaghetti nut
courted pretty Nettie Cutt.
They wed and Ed and Nettie got
a cottage in Connecticut.

Eddie said to Nettie, "Hot
spaghetti I've just got to get."
So Nettie put it in a pot
and cooked spaghetti hot and wet.

Nettie cut spaghetti up
for Eddie in Connecticut.
Eddie slurped it from a cup,
that hot spaghetti Nettie cut.

Then Eddie, Nettie and their cat
that Nettie called Spaghettipet
all sat in the spaghetti vat—
so much for their spaghettiquette.

THE CATFISH

The catfish, far more fish than cat,
prefers a fishy habitat,
it swims about beneath a stream
and does not care for milk or cream.

The catfish can't meow or purr
and features neither claws nor fur.
It only has one simple wish,
and that's to catch a rare mousefish.

AN ANTEATER

An anteater can't eat a thing but an ant,
though an anteater would if he could,
it should be understood that an anteater would,
but an ant-eating anteater can't.

He might sample a plant but an anteater can't,
no! an anteater never succeeds,
and berries and seeds are unfit for his needs
for he can't eat a thing but an ant.

An anteater can't eat a thing but an ant,
though an anteater would if he could,
it should be understood that an anteater would
but an ant-eating anteater can't.

TWICKHAM TWEER

Shed a tear for Twickham Tweer
who ate uncommon meals,
who often peeled bananas
and then only ate the peels,
who emptied jars of marmalade
and only ate the jars,
and only ate the wrappers
from his chocolate candy bars.

Though he sometimes cooked a chicken,
Twickham only ate the bones,
he discarded scoops of ice cream
though he always ate the cones,
he'd boil a small potato
but he'd only eat the skin,
and pass up canned asparagus
to gobble down the tin.

He daily dined on apple cores
and bags of peanut shells,
on cottage cheese containers,
cellophane from caramels.
Poor Twickham Tweer passed on last year,
that odd and novel man,
when he fried an egg one morning
and then ate the frying pan.

A CERTAIN LADY KANGAROO

A certain lady kangaroo
was once an awful grouch,
she pestered everyone she knew
and fussed about her pouch.

"My pouch!" she sighed. "My pouch!" she cried.
"My pouch!" she used to pout.
"The things I've tried to keep inside
 persist in falling out.
 My makeup kit, my grooming needs,
 my toothbrush and my nailbrush,
 my credit cards and worry beads,
 my tissues and my tailbrush."

That certain lady kangaroo
tried sealing it with snaps,
with tape and twine, with gobs of glue,
with staples, strings and straps,
with paper clips and wire strands,
with putty, pins and paste,
with rivets, ropes and rubber bands,
but all were just a waste.

Today that lady kangaroo
is charming, calm and chipper,
for she went to a tailor who
equipped her with a zipper.

SADIE SNATT

I'm Sadie Snatt, I'm big and fat,
I eat the finest food
like turtle tails and salmon scales
and termites spiced and stewed,
like chicken cheeks and buzzard beaks
and pickled pigeon pies,
like French-fried fleas and bees with cheese,
tomato rat surprise.

I sup on slugs and soft-boiled bugs
and tasty toads on toast,
on donkey tongues and monkey lungs
and caterpillar roast,
on snake soufflés with mayonnaise
and millipedes in mustard,
on squirrel livers sliced in slivers,
frozen fish-eye custard.

I gobble bowls of scrambled moles
and crocodile croquettes,
of rotten eggs and lizard legs
and earthworm omelettes.
I'm Sadie Snatt, I'm big and fat,
I feast on frog fondue,
and if you're nice and ask me twice,
I'll share my meal with you.

SAUCY LITTLE OCELOT

Saucy little ocelot
    ocelot
        ocelot
You like to turn and toss a lot
    toss a lot
        ocelot
You often fret and fuss a lot
    fuss a lot
        ocelot
Speckled, spotted
    polka-dotted
Saucy little ocelot

Saucy little ocelot
    ocelot
       ocelot
You're often mean and cross a lot
    cross a lot
       ocelot
You want to be the boss a lot
    boss a lot
       ocelot
Bossy, brassy
    cross and sassy
Saucy little ocelot

THE GHOSTLY GROCER OF GRUMBLE GROVE

In Grumble Grove, near Howling Hop,
there stands a nonexistent shop
within which sits, beside his stove,
the ghostly grocer of Grumble Grove.

There on rows of spectral shelves
chickens serenade themselves,
sauces sing to salted butter,
onions weep and melons mutter,

Cornflakes flutter, float on air
with loaves of bread that are not there,
thin spaghettis softly scream
and curdle quarts of quiet cream.

Phantom figs and lettuce specters
dance with cans of fragrant nectars,
sardines saunter down their aisle,
tomatoes march in single file,

A cauliflower poltergeist
juggles apples, thinly sliced,
a sausage skips on ghostly legs
as raisins romp with hard-boiled eggs.

As pea pods play with prickly pears,
the ghostly grocer sits and stares
and watches all within his trove,
that ghostly grocer of Grumble Grove.

HUFFER AND CUFFER

Huffer, a giant ungainly and gruff,
encountered a giant called Cuffer.
Said Cuffer to Huffer, I'M ROUGH AND I'M TOUGH,
said Huffer to Cuffer, I'M TOUGHER.

They shouted such insults as BOOB and BUFFOON
and OVERBLOWN BLOWHARD and BLIMP
and BLUSTERING BLUBBER and BLOATED BALLOON
and SHATTERBRAIN, SHORTY and SHRIMP.

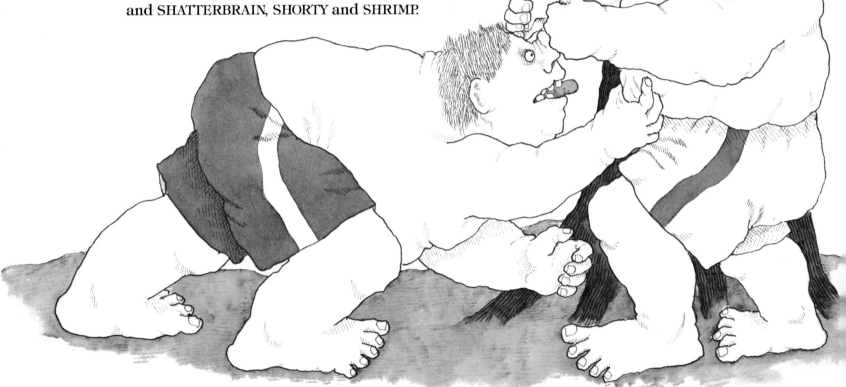

Then Huffer and Cuffer exchanged mighty blows,
they basted and battered and belted,
they chopped to the neck and they bopped in the nose,
and they pounded and pummeled and pelted.

They pinched and they punched and they smacked
    and they whacked
and they rocked and they socked and they smashed,
and they rapped and they slapped and they
    throttled and thwacked
and they thumped and they bumped and they bashed.

They cudgeled each other on top of the head
with swipes of the awfulest sort,
and now they are no longer giants, instead
they both are exceedingly short.

THE SEVEN SNEEZES OF CECIL SNEDDE

This is the saga of Cecil Snedde
whose eyes were blue, whose nose was red,
who was seized one day with a sneezing fit—
this is what happened because of it.

The first time Cecil sneezed and coughed
the sounds were indistinct and soft,
but as he sneezed and sneezed some more,
each sneeze eclipsed the sneeze before.

The second sneeze of Cecil Snedde
roused Cecil's family out of bed,
the third time Cecil sneezed that day
his next door neighbors moved away.

He tried to hold his sneezes back,
alas, he couldn't! woe! alack!
and Cecil's fourth, with awesome force,
dislodged a policeman from his horse.

His fifth produced a gusty breeze
that stripped the leaves from scores of trees,
and Cecil sneezing number six
reduced those trees to twigs and sticks.

At length there came that moment dread,
the seventh sneeze of Cecil Snedde.
Though hapless Cecil truly tried,
he could not keep that sneeze inside.

Poor Cecil Snedde... it grew and grew,
then out it burst... a great AHCHOOOOOOOOOOOOOOOOOO!
and with that final sneeze and cough
the head of Cecil Snedde flew off.